CZERNY

ONE HUNDRED PROGRESSIVE STUDIES FOR THE PIANO
Opus 139

with historical and pedagogical notes
by Matthew Edwards

T0079398

On the cover:
The Piano Lesson (1871)
by George Goodwin Kilburne
(1839–1924)

ISBN 978-1-5400-1237-1

G. SCHIRMER, *Inc.*

DISTRIBUTED BY

www.musicsalesclassical.com
www.halleonard.com

Contact Us:
Hal Leonard
7777 West Bluemound Road
Milwaukee, WI 53213
Email: info@halleonard.com

In Europe contact:
Hal Leonard Europe Limited
Distribution Centre, Newmarket Road
Bury St Edmunds, Suffolk, IP33 3YB
Email: info@halleonardeurope.com

In Australia contact:
Hal Leonard Australia Pty. Ltd.
4 Lentara Court
Cheltenham, Victoria, 3192 Australia
Email: info@halleonard.com.au

CONTENTS

**One Hundred Progressive Studies
for the Piano, Op. 139**
Part 2

HISTORICAL NOTES

CARL CZERNY (1791–1857)

Although born into a rather humble family with few prospects of prosperity or good education, Carl Czerny is today a household name, well-known to pianists around the world. Through good fortune, and a degree of talent, he interacted with some of the most important names in both Classical and Romantic literature. The list of his contacts is nearly unbelievable: he studied with Beethoven and Clementi; taught Liszt, Thalberg, and Leschetizky; and associated with countless others including Chopin, Constanze Mozart (Mozart's wife), Franz Xaver Süssmayer (Mozart's pupil), Andreas Streiche (the piano manufacturer), and many more. He was the first—or at least one of the first—to perform many of Beethoven's works, and wrote original compositions of such popularity in his day, that publishers were willing to print anything he submitted. Very often, they did not even care to hear or see it before the contract was signed.

Without doubt, Czerny lived in interesting times, and was privileged to observe first-hand the transition from the Classicism of Haydn and Mozart to the passion of the Romantics. Of course, none other than Ludwig van Beethoven was his guide through this most significant progression. Czerny stood as an observer at the crossroads of these two styles, but he also saw—and, to a great degree, assisted in—the transformation of keyboard technique. By the combination of the fame of his publications, and his successful teaching career, he became one of the foremost authorities on piano playing during this time. Even today, his legacy is sustained by his multiple collections of exercises and pedagogical works. Though his life is primarily summarized by these, a thorough study would reveal a man of many skills and interests.

Czerny's grandfather was a violinist, and his father, Wenzel Czerny (1750–1832), played several instruments, including piano, organ, and oboe. Wenzel did not marry until 1786, delayed by his fifteen years of service in the army.[1] Carl, who would be the couple's only child, was born in Vienna, Austria, on February 21, 1791. The family briefly moved to Poland, but returned to Vienna in 1795, where his father began a moderately successful career of piano teaching and piano maintenance.

It is no surprise, then, that Carl was attracted to the piano early on; his autobiography states that he began playing at the age of three, and by seven was also composing.[2] His parents kept him close to home, generally removed from most of his would-be playmates, providing ample opportunity for his musical interests. In addition, much of his education came from his father's piano students, who, as part of their lesson fees, tutored Carl in a variety of subjects including French, German, and literature. Yet about this relative isolation, he states that he "never missed the friendship of other boys, and never went out without my father."[3]

His father's skill as a pianist and teacher was at least good enough to give young Carl an excellent foundation in technique and sight-reading. He describes it thus:

> My father had no intention whatever of making a superficial virtuoso out of me; rather, he strove to develop my sight-reading ability through continuous study of new works and thus to develop my musicianship. When I was barely ten I was already able to play cleanly and fluently nearly everything by Mozart, Clementi, and the other piano composers of the time; owing to my excellent musical memory I mostly performed without the music. Whatever money my father could set aside from the scant pay for his lessons was spent on music for me...[4]

Perhaps the critical moment in the life of Carl Czerny was his introduction to Beethoven. One of Beethoven's closest friends was a man named Wenzel Krumpholz, who also happened to be a friend of the Czerny family. Through Krumpholz, Carl became aware of the great composer, and as soon as he was able, began playing as much of his music as he could find. Impressed by the 10-year old's pianism and musicality, Krumpholz agreed to take the boy and his father to Beethoven's home for a formal introduction.

The apartment was high above the street, and was rather unkempt and disheveled. Other musicians were there rehearsing, but they quickly became an impromptu audience for Carl as he sat down at Beethoven's piano to play. He performed the first movement of Mozart's C major piano concerto (K. 503), and Beethoven's own recently released Pathétique Sonata. When he finished, Beethoven uttered the words that quite possibly set Czerny's future success in motion: "The boy is talented, I myself want to teach him, and I accept him as my pupil. Let him come several times a week."[5]

Although the lessons lasted little more than a year due to Beethoven's growing need to focus on composition and the Czernys' financial situation, the relationship continued to grow until Beethoven's death in 1827. Czerny often worked closely with him, even writing the piano reduction for the publication of *Fidelio*. He also taught piano to Beethoven's nephew Carl, and gave widely successful early performances of Beethoven's works.

Performing never took a central role in Czerny's career—in fact, he cancelled his very first concert tour in 1805 even though it was supported by Beethoven himself![6] Instead, he turned his attention to teaching and composing, and found significant success in both areas. For many years, he taught twelve hours daily, and, by means of his prominent reputation, was able to charge very well for the instruction. While it was common for him to teach many of the most talented young people of the day, at least one eclipsed them all. Czerny describes the first meeting like this:

One morning in 1819… a man brought a small boy about eight years of age to me and asked me to let that little fellow play for me. He was a pale, delicate-looking child and while playing swayed on the chair as if drunk so that I often thought he would fall to the floor. Moreover, his playing was completely irregular, careless, and confused, and he had so little knowledge of correct fingering that he threw his fingers over the keyboard in an altogether arbitrary fashion. Nevertheless, I was amazed by the talent with which Nature had equipped him.[7]

Rarely does one hear such a dismal description of the great Franz Liszt, but such was Czerny's first impression. Over the next fourteen months, he worked with the boy every evening, requiring him to learn rapidly and work tirelessly on technical exercises including Czerny's own works.[8]

If we combine Czerny's published and unpublished works, his compositions number more than 1,000. He wrote symphonies, variations, arrangements, chamber works, and sacred choral works in addition to his numerous pedagogical works. Not all of his music was received well—in particular, Schumann's review of a piano work entitled *The Four Seasons* stated that "it would be hard to discover a greater bankruptcy in imagination than Czerny has proved."[9] Harsh, to be sure, but many of the greatest pianists, including Liszt and Chopin, played his works throughout the continent, to great acclaim. To this day, many of the sonatas are regularly performed.

Professionally, Czerny's reputation remained generally high throughout his life. Personally, however, he remained alone, never marrying. His brief autobiography, which describes his life to 1842, ends rather abruptly with the following sentence: "In 1827 I lost my mother and five years later (1832) my father, and was thus left all alone, since I have no relatives whatever."

Carl Czerny died on July 15, 1857. A humble beginning, a quiet passing; but in between, a remarkable life.

PERFORMANCE NOTES

Introduction to Czerny's Music

Czerny organized his compositions for piano into four main categories:

- Studies and exercises
- Easy pieces for students
- Brilliant pieces for concerts
- Serious music[10]

He is best known for his pedagogical and technical works, yet he also wrote many compositional treatises. He seems to have held to the idea that performance and composition should go hand in hand, and even expressed disappointment that Liszt had not had sufficient instruction from him in composition.[11] He was a pedagogue at heart, and sought through all of his works to teach and admonish young musicians.

100 Progressive Studies for the Piano, Op. 139

This collection is an excellent addition to any student's library as they move toward greater skill in their keyboard studies. Aimed primarily at an intermediate level, the works contain no octave playing, thereby accommodating younger pianists as well.

There is a general increase in difficulty and type of technique throughout the volume, but the pieces do not necessarily need to be taken in strict order. Because of the wide variety of technical elements, one may choose to select whichever exercises apply to a student's current technical struggles.

Indeed the large number of technical elements covered makes this possibly one of the best books for the intermediate-level student. From simple *legato* and *staccato* playing, to repeated notes, double thirds and more, this book covers nearly every element one could encounter in piano literature of a similar level.

General Suggestions

This publication should be approached with purpose; it is not meant to be simply a required element of lessons, or a set of mundane "drills" to add an extra few minutes onto practice time. The goal for each exercise should be to learn good technique and fundamental musicality. Speed is at all times secondary to these two items. With the proper attention to good technique, speed will follow on its own. I frequently mention technique in my commentary on the individual pieces, and have attempted to clarify certain approaches to the keyboard that have proven extremely useful to me and to my students. However, it is understandably difficult to convey the subtleties of piano technique in just a few words.

Clarity and Evenness

The pieces in this publication should be played clearly and evenly. It is typically a sign of a technical problem if there is an unexpected accent or rhythmic unevenness in a scale or arpeggio. It is most important, in order to overcome this problem, that the fingers and hand (and by extension, the entire body) stay relaxed; by tensing your muscles, everything becomes more difficult. In addition, focusing on this element trains the ear to listen carefully, and encourages good practice habits.

Fingering

Remember that the fingerings given here are suggestions only. Every hand is different, so every fingering should be examined; don't try to force a fingering that may not work for you!

I would suggest that the printed fingering should always be attempted first. If it doesn't work, look for an alternative, using the following ideas to guide your choices:

- A relaxed hand: in most cases, try to keep the fingers close together, and the hand moving as a unit. This more easily allows the fingers to stay relaxed, and the hand to move both faster and more smoothly. Of course, stretches are required when extending to the octave and beyond (of the sixth, for smaller hands), but allow the hand to move toward the extended note, keeping the fingers relaxed.

- Economy of motion: this applies to the fingers alone, as well as to the entire hand. Simply put, it is the idea of minimizing the number of crossovers in a passage—grouping as many notes into one hand position as possible. Imagine for example, if a simple C-major arpeggio over three octaves were played with only the first and second fingers; there would be several hand positions, creating a much more difficult passage.

Tempos

Metronome markings are not included in the majority of printed editions. The primary focus should be the improvement of technique, and learning how to deal with certain technical issues—both pianistic and physical. I have seen too many students practice for hours, pursuing a metronomic goal with tunnel vision, ignoring the fact that their physical approach may not ever allow them to achieve top speed. Indeed, this is not to say that fast tempos should be avoided, by any means. Rather, they must be approached carefully. Each student should play the faster pieces as quickly and as cleanly as good technique will allow.

Ornamentation

The graces, namely, the shake, the turn, the appoggiatura, etc., are the flowers of music; and the clear, correct, and delicate execution of them, embellishes and exalts every melody and every passage. But, when they are played stiff, hard, or unintelligibly, they may rather be compared to blots of ink or spots of dirt.[12]

A great deal of research and opinion are available on this topic. While it is important to be familiar with the current conventional wisdom, one cannot forget the fundamental principle that ornaments, as Czerny himself said above, are decorative and improvisatory. They are decorative in the sense that they are subservient to the primary line, and improvisatory in that their execution varies—slightly or greatly—from performer to performer. In the Baroque era, Johann Sebastian Bach created a very detailed chart, explaining the ornamentation written in his works.

However, Sandra Rosenblum, in her extremely helpful book *Performance Practices in Classic Piano Music* states that "Neither Haydn, Mozart, nor Beethoven left any systematic instructions for the performance of ornaments."[13] Clementi is perhaps the most significant composer to write instructions on ornamentation, yet Rosenblum further states that "Although many treatises discussed ornaments and gave instructions for their performance, there was not—and is not now—complete agreement regarding either notation or performance."[14] The point to be seen here is that while there may be some general "rules" about the execution of turns, trills, and appoggiaturas, there are still many valid variables left to the unique and instinctive choice of each performer.

Musicality

These works are miniature creations, and by the simple fact of their brevity, do not contain excessively deep musical thoughts. However, they can be used to learn countless basic principles, such as shaping a line, closing a phrase, planning the dynamic architecture of a work, and of course, following the printed markings. Strive to make each piece as musical as possible.

Notes on Selected Exercises

Nos. 1–10

The first ten exercises in the book are indeed generally the easiest of the set, although not without a few elements that younger students may struggle with. General technical elements covered include beginning Alberti patterns, left-hand accompaniment patterns, lyrical right-hand passage playing, all with relatively minimal difficulty.

Perhaps the more difficult items would include parallel thirds in Nos. 1, 4, and 8, and the left-hand tremolo pattern in No. 9. Although it could seem early to introduce such elements, I believe students should be encouraged to try these fingerings. Playing thirds like this can certainly help students focus on rounded fingers, as it is much more difficult to play them with flat fingers. Additionally, thirds help build independence of the fingers. An alternative to using the suggested fingering, would be to use the same fingering for each third. This type of technique—similar to octave technique—will be covered in multiple locations throughout the book. For the tremolo pattern, treat the interval as a "single unit," by balancing the fingers equally over each note.

No. 11

Double thirds here are fingered identically, and will therefore require a relaxed wrist. This is an excellent introduction to octave technique. Keep the wrist free of tension as it drops into each third, and moves up or down the keyboard.

Nos. 12–14

The left hand has a consistent broken-chord accompaniment in each of these; keep it steady and without accent. Focus on a well-shaped musical line, balanced well above the left hand. Keep the grace notes of No. 12 light, and unobtrusive.

No. 15

Though the rhythmic patterns have indeed changed hands compared to the previous three exercises, the melodic element can still be seen in the right hand. The first, or highest note of each triplet is typically the important one.

Nos. 16 & 18

Two fingering options are presented for the parallel sixths: using fingers 5 and 1 for all, or phrasing the top voice. These fingering options can be attempted to arrive at what works best for different size hands. Both are marked Andantino, so there is no pressure to play these with any great speed.

No. 17

A good workout for the left hand, this is predominantly a study in the Alberti bass pattern. With the melody in the right hand, this exercise is clearly helpful for many Classical-era works that students may be studying.

No. 19

This is excellent practice for scales and other passages. Musically, focus on the "conversation" between the hands, as the left hand is more than just accompaniment.

No. 20

A good early study in syncopated playing between the hands. In such cases, always focus most on the notes that land ON the beat, and the offbeat notes will more naturally land precisely between the beats.

Nos. 21, 23, 24, & 31

At first glance, these appear to be just a melody and an accompaniment pattern. However, Czerny has placed half notes in the left hand, creating a subtle bass line. This should not be specifically emphasized, as holding the note is in itself enough for us to hear

the line. Treat it almost as a harmonization with the melody. No. 23 adds a few ornaments in the form of turns. These could begin directly on beat two, lasting a quarter, or on the "and" of two, lasting an eighth note.

No. 22

There are several right-hand crossovers here. Be careful to cross smoothly, rather than suddenly, so that the lower notes are not accented. This way, they provide a simple, but clear foundation to the harmony.

No. 25

This exercise almost doesn't have a single focus element, containing echo dynamics, Alberti bass, varying articulations, etc. Pay careful attention that the sixteenth-note figures are exactly together, as in measures 1, 3, etc.

No. 26

Think of this as a duet between the hands; the left hand is nearly equal to the right. Keep the focus on both, all the way through the cadences.

No. 27

This is the first work to prominently feature repeated notes. The fingering here suggests using the same finger for each note; again, a relaxed wrist is necessary. This is good preparation for octave study. I would recommend trying it this way, rather than adjusting to the "standard" fingering of 3-2-1.

No. 28

Thirds are back again here, in a comfortable "handful"; excellent practice for curved fingers and future scales in thirds.

No. 29

This exercise is nearly a study in rhythmic contrasts. I suggest choosing a tempo based on the left hand, but keeping in mind that the resulting relatively slower right hand will require careful focus on the longer line.

No. 30

Relaxed hand and wrist is at the focus again, as the dotted eighth-sixteenth patterns will require it for clarity. The fingered thirds are also pushed to be a bit faster, being part of the dotted pattern in the right hand.

No. 32

The standard chromatic fingering is introduced in this study. Be careful to observe that the very first scale is not purely chromatic at the end.

No. 33

This would be a good preparation for turns, although that ornament has already shown up in a previous exercise. The figure in measure 1 isn't exactly executed as a typical turn, but is at least similar, and adds a nice *staccato* before landing on the dotted quarter. A delicate sound in this figure is the focus here.

No. 34

Multiple ornaments are presented here; a slow tempo is quite appropriate for practicing them. Trills could first be played rhythmically, and eventually, faster. According to *The New Grove Dictionary of Music and Musicians*, the figure in measure 14 would be called a trill, a *pralltriller*, or a *schneller*. The latter pair of terms indicate a brief ornament, begun ON the given pitch, rising one above, and returning. It would also seem, in the context of this eighth-note line, that the ornament should begin on the beat, rather than before. However, playing it before the beat could also be argued, as Czerny indicated in several examples in his *School of Embellishments*, Op. 355.

No. 35

This is an unusual little exercise, but seems to focus on the leaping right-hand line, possibly in preparation for broken octaves, as seen in measure 17. The accent leads the student toward emphasis on the upper note, as is often the case in such figures.

No. 36

This exercise hints at the rapid scale passages to be found in Czerny's *School of Velocity*, Op. 299; the fingerings are all standard major-scale fingerings.

No. 37

This is an excellent exercise on finger crossing, utilizing a figure that turns on itself as it moves up and down the keyboard. Practice measures 9–12 carefully, as the leap after the turn is larger than at the beginning.

No. 38

Another drill for thirds, even almost hinting at a trill in thirds. Keep the fingers rounded, and wrist level above the keys.

No. 39

The turns in measures 1–8 could begin on the quarter note (beats 2 and 4) or on the eighth note after those beats. Beginning at measure 10, there is even less time to complete the turn. One option

would be to begin on the "and" of 1, and finish on 2, then moving on to the next eighth note; personally, this would be my preference. Alternatively, the turn could start right on beat 1, and end on beat 2, before moving on to the next eighth note; the turn is slower this way, and may be easier to play musically.

No. 40

Focus on a light, bouncing *staccato* here. The grace notes should not be prominent or take too much attention from the larger notes. Play them nearly simultaneously with the note to which they are attached.

No. 41

The right-hand figure is, in a way, a study on the two-note slur, yet with many different configurations. Keep the hand light, and remember the "drop-lift" standard of the slur; even at a higher speed, that can still be maintained.

No. 42

There are two excellent uses for this exercise. First, and most obvious, is as a study/preparation for trills. Every adjacent finger option is presented here. Second, for the parallel trills between the hands in measures 9, 11, and 13, listen carefully to keep them exactly together.

No. 43

This piece takes a further step with the parallel trills from No. 42. Not only are the parallel sixteenth-notes now moving over 3 notes instead of 2, one must also hold down a whole or half note at the same time. Be very sure to hold that note down with minimal pressure—really, just the weight of that finger! Otherwise, the tension caused by continued deep pressure will make the sixteenths very difficult to manage. From this perspective, the piece is also a study in independence of the fingers.

No. 44

At the beginning, the right hand must maintain two voices at once, shaping the upper as the melody, and the lower as a rhythmic accompaniment. Eventually, the left hand has a similar passage. Take care to treat each line individually, and don't let the "second voice" become too loud, like a simple drumbeat.

No. 45

The risk here for the left hand is that it will soon tire, and begin grasping at the keys, causing the rhythm of the triplets to become uneven. Try not to think of the broken chord element, but rather of each note as it ascends the chord. Also, try focusing slightly on the second note of each group; concentration on the first can often lead to the figure sounding "bunched up."

No. 46
Here we have a brief introduction to arpeggios, most with all white notes, and one with a black note in the middle. The left-hand accompaniment is simple enough to require little attention, allowing focus on a steady and even arpeggio.

No. 47
Keep the line lyrical and connected across the bar lines. The left hand should follow the shape of the right as a gentle and flowing accompaniment. In measure 15, the turn should be executed right on beat 4; perhaps the tempo should be chosen with this turn in mind. See the notes to No. 34 for a brief discussion on the *Schneller* ornament.

No. 48
Quite possibly the easiest way to teach a relaxed hand and finger position is through the use of five-finger patterns; this exercise focuses on exactly that. Allow the arm and hand to move smoothly in the direction of the pattern as the fingers simply drop into place to play the notes.

No. 49
Marked moderato, the challenge here is to keep the melodic line well shaped over the long half notes. Without doubt, the performer should sing the melody internally so that the notes do note simply pop out individually and disconnectedly, like fireflies in the night.

Nos. 50, 51
Here are yet two more examples, among many in this book, of a held lower note in the left hand. Once again, this helps draw our attention to the fact the bass line is actually a bit more than just that, and can indeed contribute to the overall musical shape of the phrases. In No. 51, the lower voice can be seen in both quarter and half note values, sounding even more nearly contrapuntal than No. 50.

No. 52
This piece is more like a study in the character of a march than a technical exercise. Keep the pulse absolutely steady and the sixteenth notes sharp.

No. 53
Roughly at the midway point, the exercises begin to grow yet more difficult. The parallel chromatic scales will require some careful work, especially if this is the first encounter with them. If possible, aim for an allegro that fits the quarter-note pulse of measure 3, rather than the sixteenth-notes of the scale passages.

No. 54
Here we find not one, but two types of cross-rhythms. Two against three is solved fairly easily, as the patterns fit together mathematically. In three against four, focus on the one beat the patterns have in common, being sure to play the first of each group together, and listening for the remaining notes to be evenly spaced over the beat. Using a traditional phrase or counting method for these work somewhat initially, but are not always absolutely correct. Beyond all of this, remember to stay focused on making music!

No. 55
The arpeggiated figures should be played before the beat, landing on the larger eighth note. Additionally, they should not sound like they are part of the melodic line, but rather a flourish that embellishes the high note.

Nos. 56–58
These three exercises focus on rapid repeated notes in varying situations. The fingerings in No. 56 may seem tricky at first, but implementing a relaxed wrist, as described before will be the key. Additionally, allowing the hand to move forward gradually helps relieve some of the tension. In Nos. 57 and 58, with the fingering provided, be very careful not to grasp at the groups of repeated notes, as this will cause the notes to sound uneven, and will create unnecessary tension in the hand and forearm. Use a slightly higher hand and wrist, and drop each finger into the keys.

No. 59
This study introduces a triplet figure that serves both as ornament and melodic line. Keep the left hand light and steady. Also be sure that each repetition of the triplet-eighth figure moves dynamically toward its ending point, usually on beat 1 of the following measure.

No. 60
Reminiscent of No. 44, this study has a clear duet between the outer voices, yet challenges the student to make the inner voice (also in the right hand) a subtle accompaniment pattern. This pattern should follow the voices dynamically, and should never have notes that sound suddenly accented.

No. 61

The pattern presented here may be one of the more recognizable figures from the Classical era. It is seen frequently in both Mozart and Haydn, and this short study will be an excellent preparation for those and other works. The fingering in measure 13 may seem awkward at first, but is helpful for the movement of this version of the figure as it moves up the keyboard.

Nos. 62, 63, & 66

With these exercises, Czerny sets the tone for the beginning of Part 2 of this collection. The focus of these is primarily musical rather than technical. No. 62 should be sung internally to keep the line flowing across the long quarter notes (nearly half notes, with the tie.) Make the left hand just as musical, as it migrates through some chromatic harmonies. No. 63 requires chord tones that sound precisely together, and are dynamically even, with a subtle emphasis on the top. No. 66, as in previous exercises, blends one of the secondary voices with the accompaniment. Listen carefully to blend the two into a lovely duet.

No. 64

Scales and broken chords are the emphasis here, often beginning on the second sixteenth note of the measure. Counting and preparation are crucial in such situations. Clarity and evenness will make this a sparkling, though brief, work.

No. 65

An Alberti-like study with a leaping *staccato* melody. Even with the larger intervals, stay attentive to the shape of the melody. Consider each note a part of it, rather than just the top or bottom of each eighth-note pair. The rolling left hand is slightly different than the expected Alberti pattern; careful not to overemphasize the middle note.

No. 67

Chromatic thirds can often feel quite crowded in the hand, so it is of utmost importance that the fingers be rounded, and the hand well over the keys. As always, drop the thirds into the keys, not holding any tension in the fingers; the *staccato* marking should help with this. When the notes become *legato*, continue playing them in the same manner.

No. 68

A more extended arpeggio study using predominantly first inversion arpeggios in the right hand. Watch the dynamics closely, especially the *decrescendo* in measures 9 and 11. In measure 15, drop the chords equally weighted into the keys, keeping the wrist relaxed as always.

No. 69

The left hand has the melody here with somewhat of a countermelody in the right hand. Make the left-hand tone deep and full, as the right hand adds an interesting harmonic setting.

No. 70

This is more of a broken chord study than an arpeggio study. When playing groups of broken chords, never "grab" the notes—especially the first two or three of each figure. "Grabbing" always makes an uneven sound. Instead, play each note distinctly, moving the hand forward through each of the four notes, then returning back slightly to begin the next set.

No. 71

The same motion described above for No. 70 is applicable here as well, although for a slightly different figure. Move forward through this figure, being sure that each note is clear, distinct, and even.

No. 72

Another military-style march, but at a softer dynamic this time. The hands are further apart as well, and will require less from the left hand to achieve a proper balance.

No. 73

Large melodic intervals naturally have dramatic tension. Beyond focusing on the technical difficulties of making these leaps, be sure to connect the melodic notes musically. Do not allow the note before a leap to be accented or the line will most definitely be broken.

No. 74

This cross-hand piece sounds like a vocal duet in which the right hand plays both parts. Keep the upper line lyrical and sweet, and in contrast with the lower voice's deeper, fuller tone.

No. 75

This work is predominantly a five-finger study in even left-hand playing. Move the hand forward through the first beat, and return during the second. The right hand adds a dramatic element within broken chord sections.

No. 76

This work is almost a study in reading accidentals, as the right hand plays both melodic and harmonic minor passages over a somewhat more chromatic progression. The fingering given here for the descending harmonic minor scales is slightly different than you may expect, but is effective in this particular setting.

Between Nos. 76 and 77, Czerny has placed a chart that identifies all major chords and their relative minor chords. It might be a helpful reference, a study sheet, or a quick way to instill muscle and/or sight memory by playing and identifying each chord.

No. 77

This is the longest exercise by far to this point, and multiple technical difficulties from the earlier works are combined into a single study. Therefore, perhaps it should be considered more of an etude, with the focus being not only on the technical, but also the musical.

No. 78

The melodic line is quite fragmented in this piece, so once again, singing internally to connect across the pauses is critical. It should not be taken too quickly, and allow the left hand to create a sense of drama as it helps shape the musical line.

No. 79

The double trills in this work could be played parallel, or simply as two fast trills together, not necessarily lining up. Slower parallel trills may be best however, especially when practicing left-hand trills for the first time. Notice the quick *decrescendo* as the trills end the first two times.

No. 80

Don't let the quarter notes fool you; this is a very fast piece! Keep the hands light and relaxed, especially in the accompaniment. The right hand should be clear above the left, and point dynamically to the end of each long phrase.

No. 81

The sixteenth notes in the opening of this study should be as graceful as ornaments, but still sound like part of the melody; in other words, don't simply throw away the notes. Be sure to count this in two, rather than six to give it the lilting feel of dotted quarters, without heaviness on each eighth note. This is further enhanced by a graceful right hand.

No. 82

Many double-note passages are featured here as melodic or counter-melodic elements. Allegretto is an appropriate tempo; anything faster will cloud the clarity of the double notes. In measure 19, trill only the upper note, not both.

No. 83

More than an E-flat scale study alone, this contains a great deal of broken interval playing. Be careful to keep the lower right-hand note balanced as a duet with the left hand in measures 9 and following. Measure 17 presents a somewhat new technical element; focus on the note that plays on the beat, thereby helping the offbeat notes to be steady.

No. 84

Depending on the speed chosen, the thirty-second notes could be rather short. Be sure they are played with clarity, and not as if "snapped" by the fingers. Notice that the *crescendo* markings tend to follow these passages, indicating that all notes increase in volume gradually, not just the longer ones.

No. 85

The dotted quarter notes provide a clear and steady pulse in this piece. Sixteenth notes should be as graceful as possible, almost floating above the left hand, and always moving toward the final note of the phrase.

No. 86

Another broken interval study, although different from No. 83 in that the melody is the higher of the two notes. In this case, be careful not to let the left-hand thumb play too loudly, breaking up the line.

Nos. 87, 89, 90, and 92

These pieces are studies on enharmonicism. Each begins in a flat key, then changes to the enharmonic sharp key. The unique element is that a portion of the music in the new key is simply a respelling of the same portion in the original key. Having first learned the music in the original key, students will hear the same music as they read in the enharmonic key. This is a very clever way to introduce some of the more difficult keys.

Though these works contain mostly technical elements already encountered in the book, it is worth noting that No. 87 is very chordal, and students should focus on balanced sound and voicing.

No. 88

Keep the right hand and wrist relaxed for the repeated chords. Care should be taken to keep these chords under the left-hand melody dynamically. In the second half, this focus shifts a bit toward the right hand, as it contains the more melodic element in the top part of the chords.

No. 91

Similar to No. 59, the triplet figure should again be light and graceful. Despite the rests that separate the figures, they do comprise the melody of this piece, but should sound connected musically.

No. 93

Grazioso ed espressivo is the perfect description here, revealing both the character and the focus of the study. Let the sixteenth and thirty-second notes glide lightly up and down the keys, always pointing to their final longer note, or phrase ending. Even at a generally softer dynamic level, the melody should be in the foreground. Remember also that the *sforzando* markings indicate a moment that is simply louder than its surroundings, and not a sudden jump to *forte*.

No. 94

This work presents the typical Classical-era Alberti bass/right-hand melody setting in sixteenths and thirty-second notes, as opposed to the "slower" rhythms in the earlier part of the book. This does not significantly change the outcome of the sound, but does prepare one for other works written with these more complicated rhythms.

No. 95

This trill study focuses on longer trills for both hands, although not simultaneously. Try to follow the given fingerings, even is some are a bit uncomfortable, such as the 5-4 trills right at the beginning. This is a difficult one, but approach it with a slight rotation of the hand and wrist as if it were a very small broken interval passage.

No. 96

The right hand's repeated notes are short, in a single set of three for each measure. Care should be taken not to accent the last of each.

No. 97–99

Alternating passages such as those presented here can often prove fiendishly difficult to keep even and steady. As stated before, it is best to focus primarily on the note that is on the beat, and the offbeat notes fall more naturally into place. This takes yet more attention when the intervals are farther apart, such as in measures 20–23 of No. 97, as our ear tends to gravitate toward the higher—and in this case, offbeat—note. For No. 98, the problem is further complicated by alternating *pairs* of notes, yet the principle still applies. Remember to rotate the hand and wrists slightly, as done in more common broken interval playing. Finally, No. 99 varies the same concept yet again, with a single left-hand note alternating with a pair of right-hand notes.

No. 100

The final study appears at first to be less difficult than many of the preceding exercises. However, it is one of the few pieces marked presto, and playing this at a truly fast tempo will indeed require careful practice. Perhaps, in a sense, this is Czerny's way of leading the student to the far more frequent presto marking found in the *School of Velocity*. At any tempo, clarity and evenness should always be more important than speed.

Notes:

[1] Little is known about his mother—she is described by Czerny simply as "a Moravian girl."

[2] Czerny, Carl. "Recollections from My Life." Trans. Ernest Sanders. *The Musical Quarterly,* Vol. 42, No. 3. (Jul., 1956), p. 303.

[3] ibid., 305.

[4] ibid., 303.

[5] ibid., 307.

[6] Stephan D. Lindeman and George Barth, "Czerny, Carl," *Grove Music Online,* ed. Laura Macy: www.grovemusic.com (accessed 1 Feb. 2011).

[7] Czerny, Carl. "Recollections from My Life." Trans. Ernest Sanders. *The Musical Quarterly,* Vol. 42, No. 3. (Jul., 1956), pp. 314–315.

[8] Alan Walker, et al, "Liszt, Franz." *Grove Music Online,* ed. Laura Macy: www.grovemusic.com (accessed 1 Feb. 2011).

[9] Stephan D. Lindeman and George Barth, "Czerny, Carl," *Grove Music Online,* ed. Laura Macy: www.grovemusic.com (accessed 1 Feb. 2011).

[10] ibid.

[11] Czerny, Carl. "Recollections from My Life." Trans. Ernest Sanders. *The Musical Quarterly,* Vol. 42, No. 3. (Jul., 1956), p. 316.

[12] Czerny, Carl. *Letters to a Young Lady, on the Art of Playing the Pianoforte.* Trans. J. A. Hamilton. (Da Capo Press: New York), 1982.

[13] Rosenblum, Sandra. *Performance Practices in Classic Piano Music* (Indiana University Press: Bloomington, 1988), p. 216.

[14] ibid., p. 217.

One Hundred Progressive Studies
for the Piano, Op. 139
Part 1

Carl Czerny
(1791–1857)

2

Allegretto

Moderato

3

Andantino

4

6

Allegretto

7

Allegretto con moto

8

Allegro

9

12

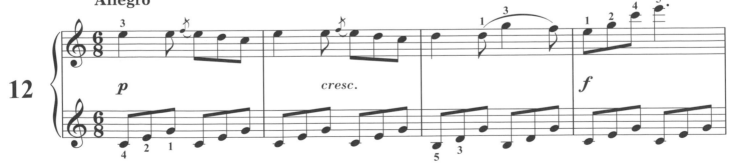

Allegro molto

14

Allegro moderato

Andantino

16

Allegro

19

Moderato

sim.

20

Andantino

22

23

Andante

Allegro

25

26

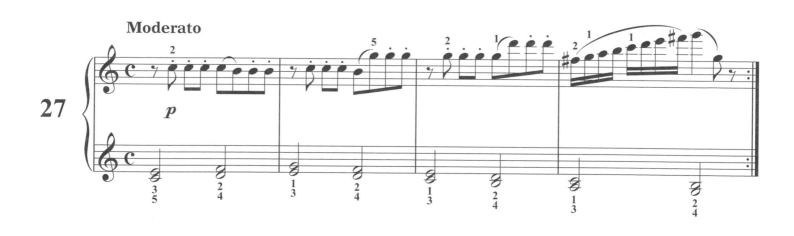

Allegro vivace

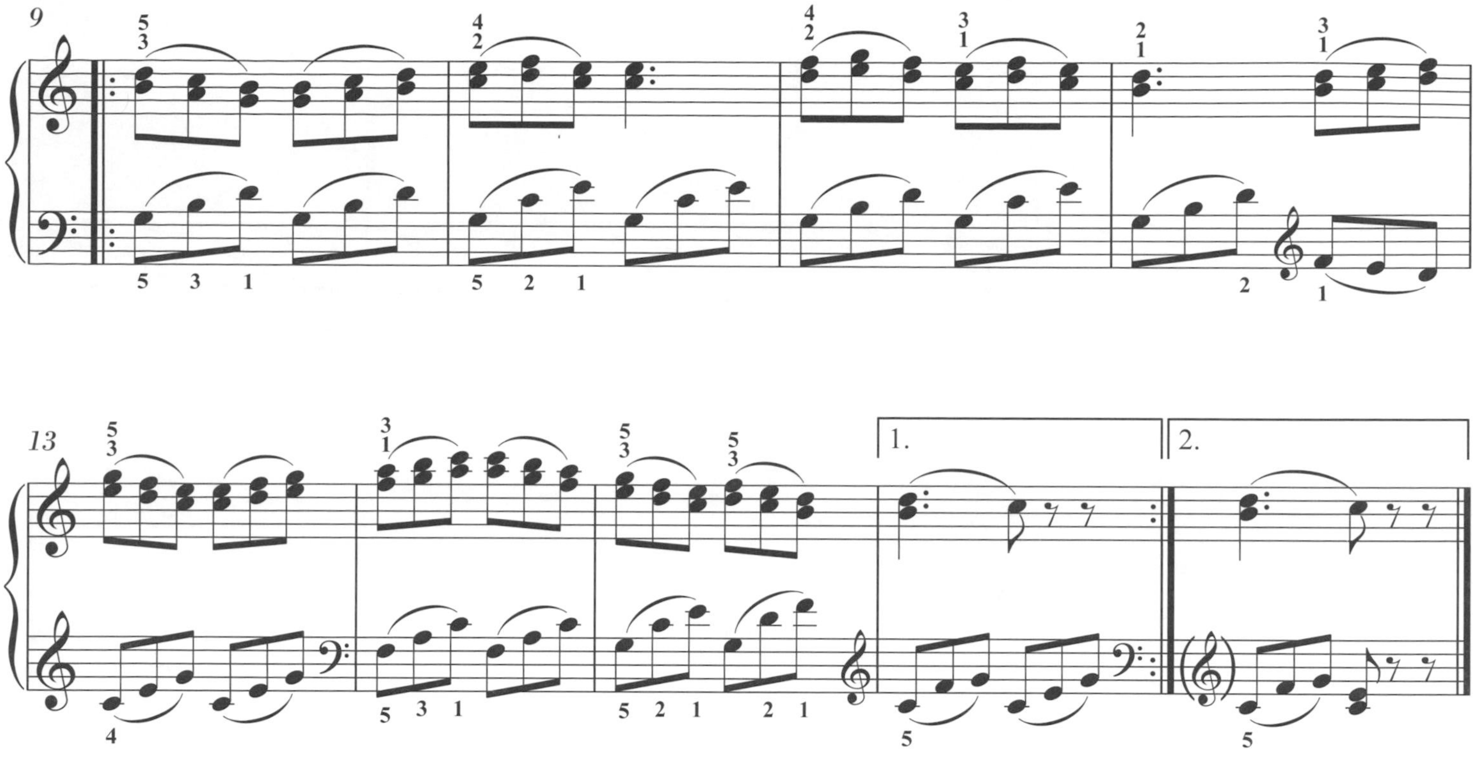

29

Allegro, quasi presto

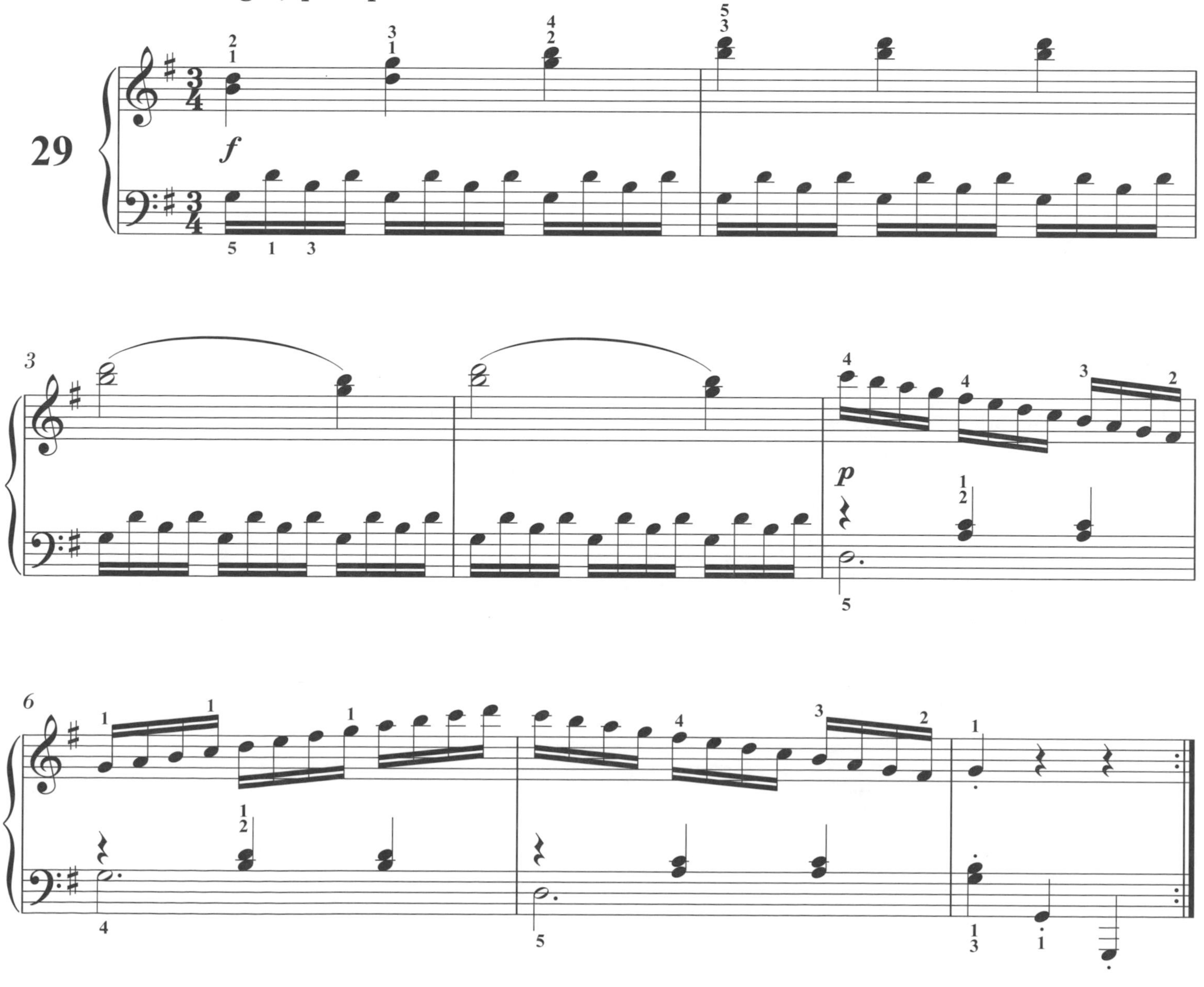

Allegro maestoso

MARCIA

30

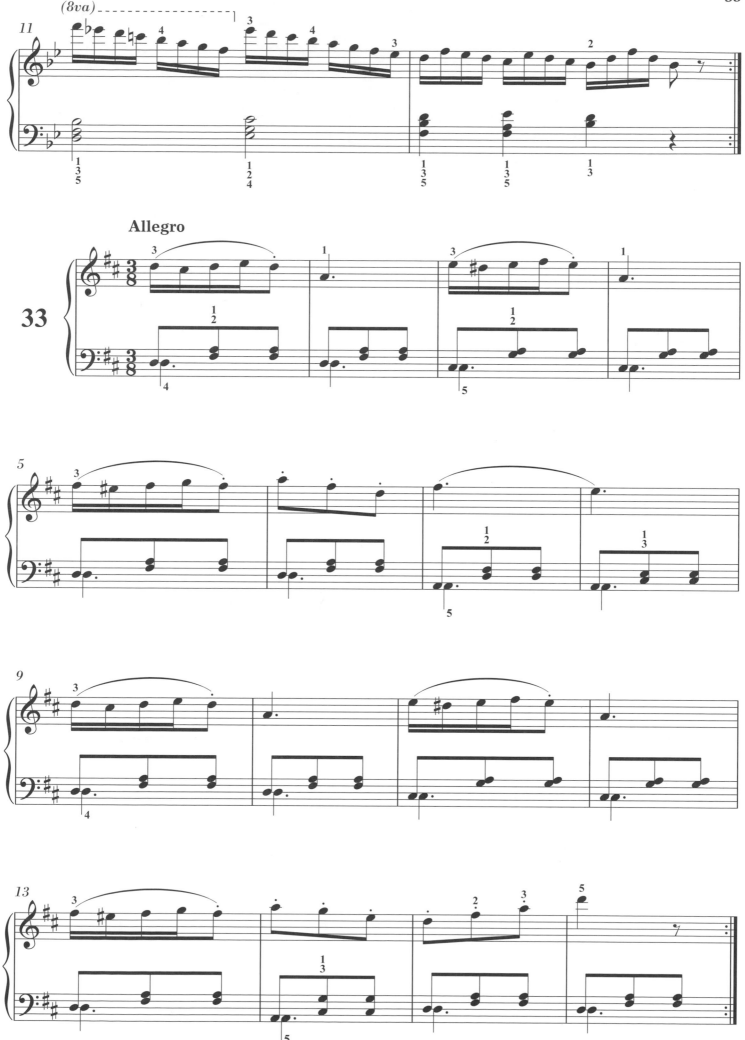

Allegro

33

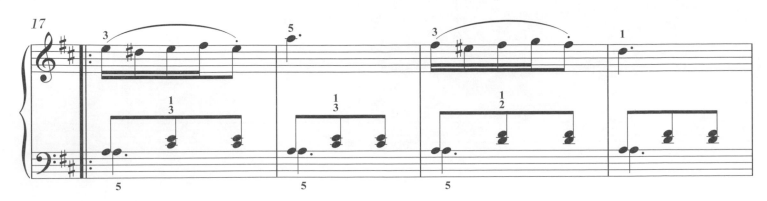

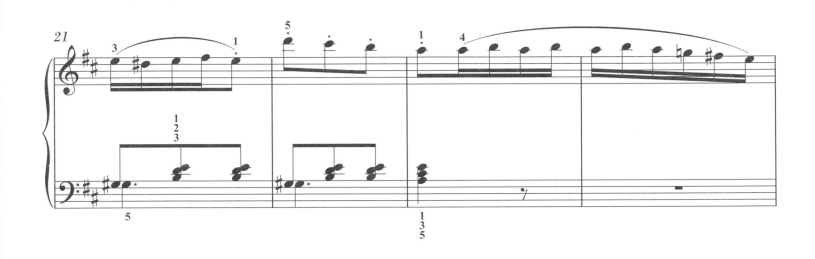

Andante espressivo

Allegro moderato

35

Allegro

38

Allegretto vivace

46

Allegro

43

Allegro moderato

44

dolce e legato

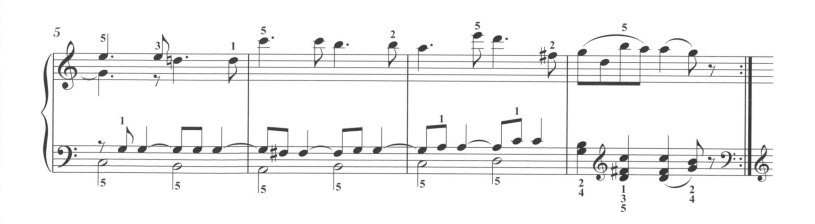

Allegro molto

45

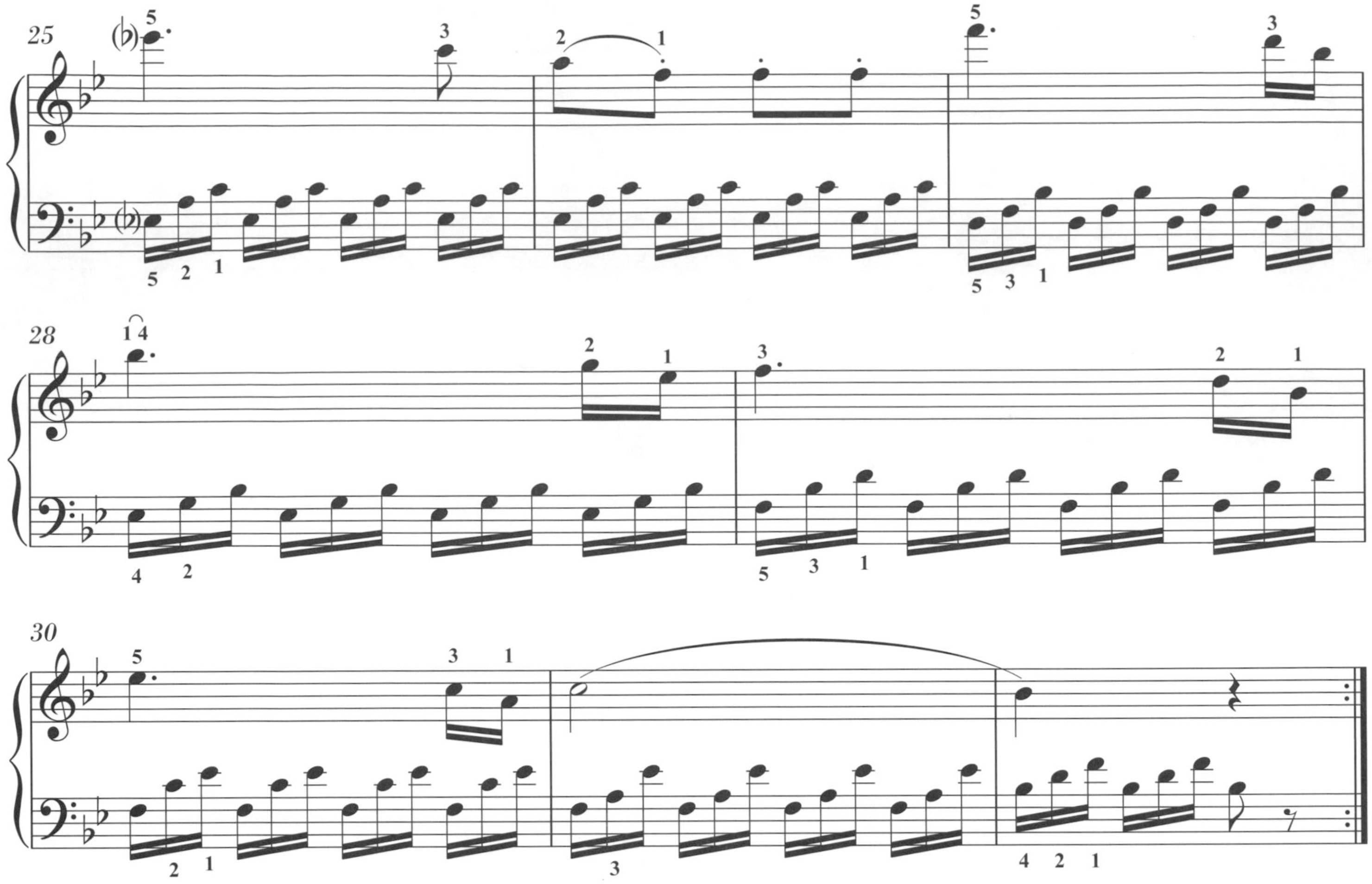

46

Allegro

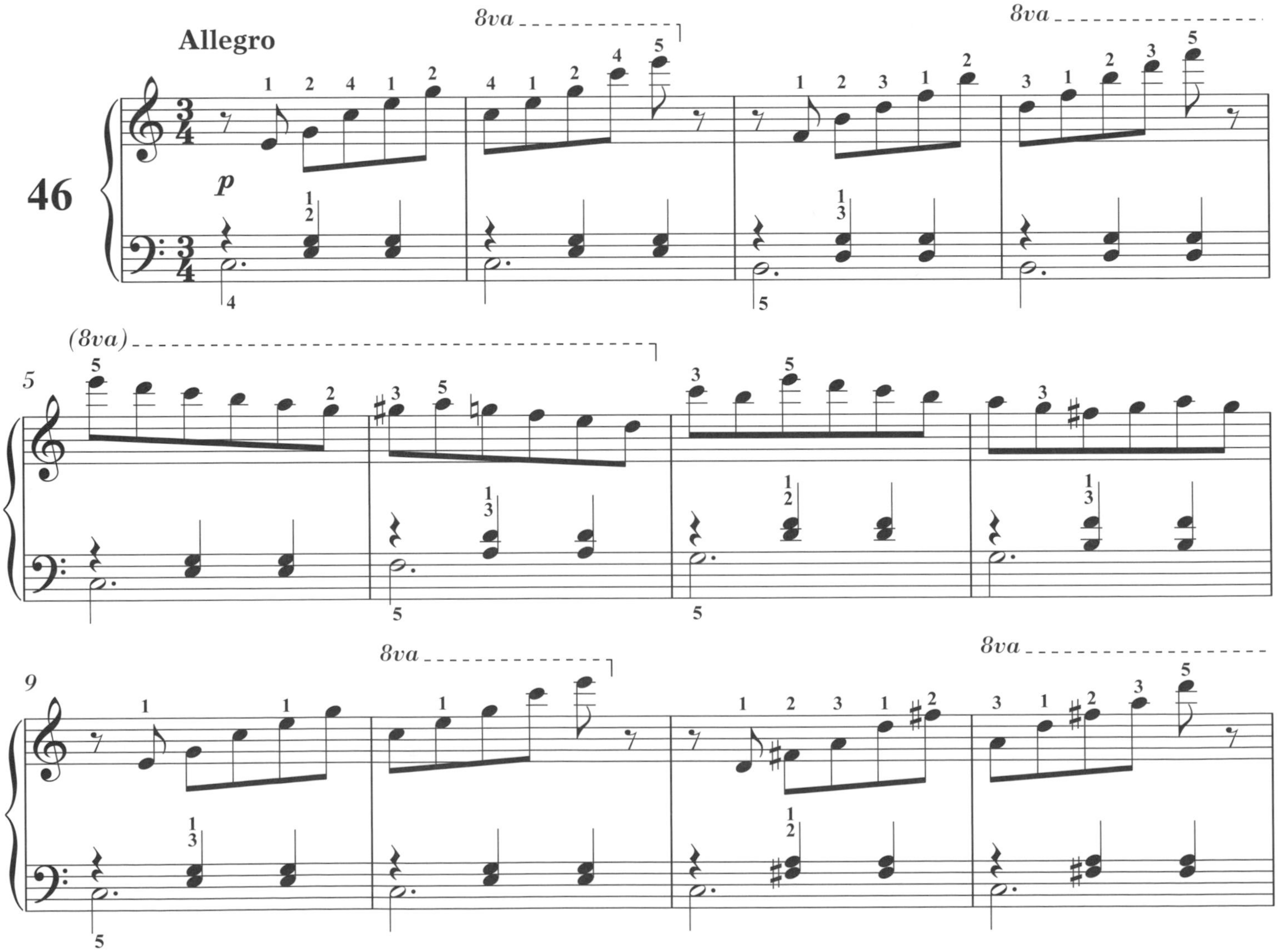

56

Allegro vivo

50

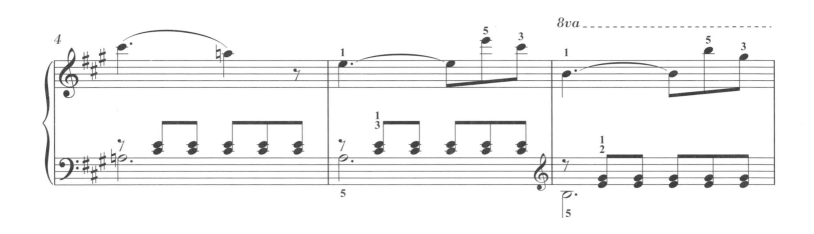

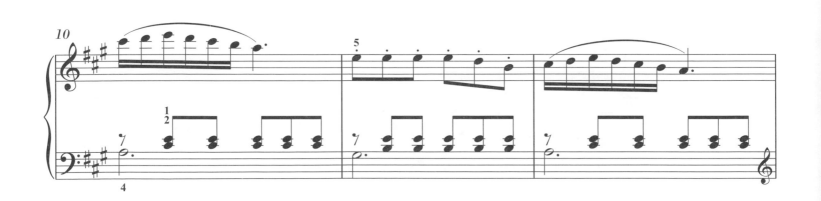

60

Moderato alla marcia

52

64

Moderato

54

Allegro moderato

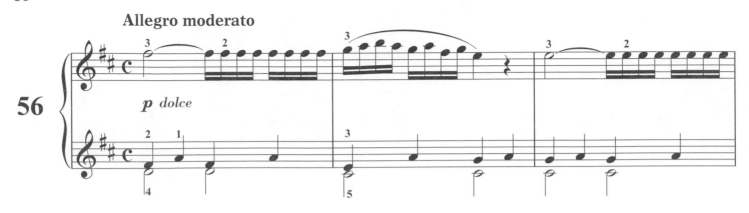

56

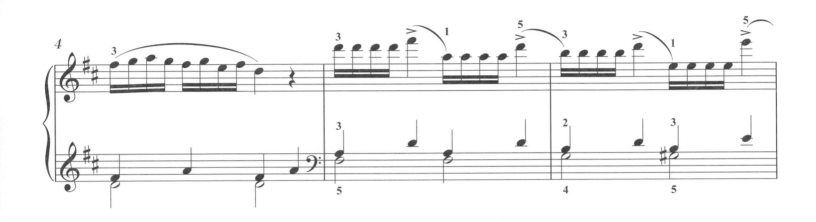

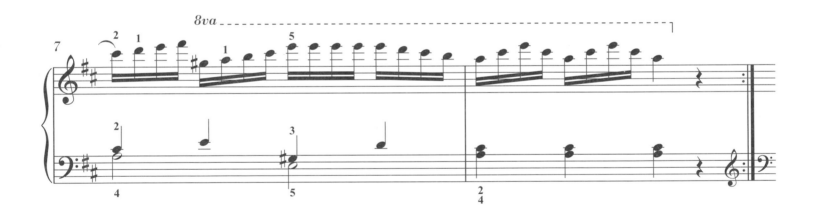

70

One Hundred Progressive Studies
for the Piano, Op. 139
Part 2

Carl Czerny
(1791–1857)

Allegretto vivace

Allegro vivo

65

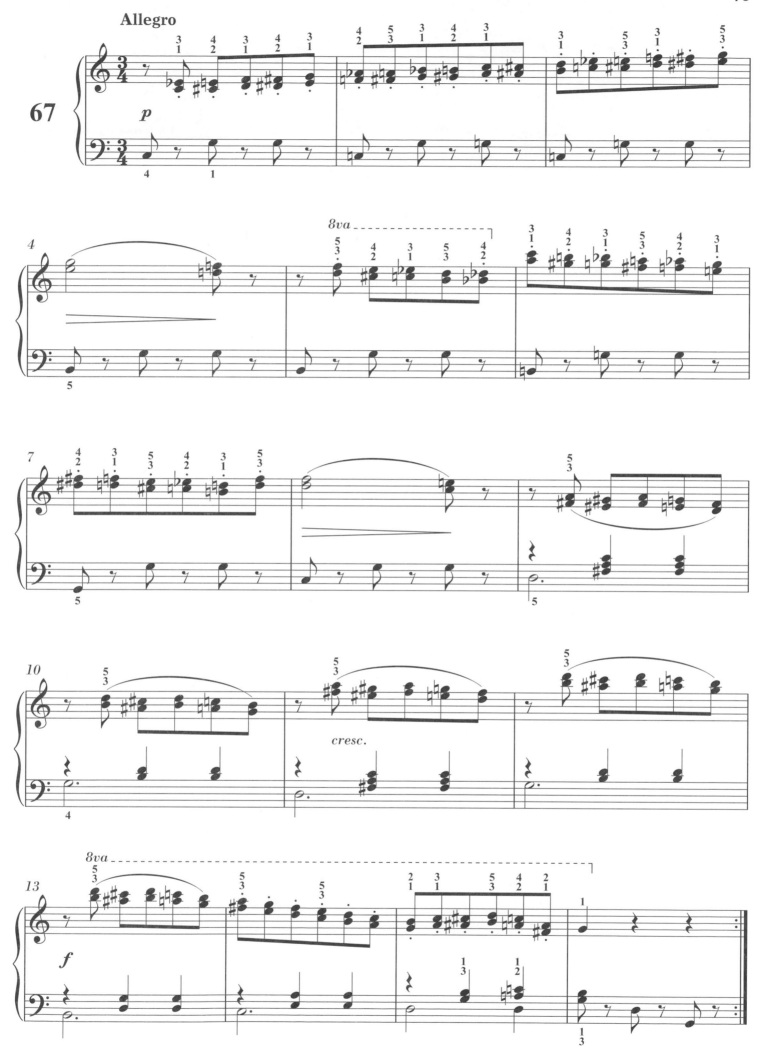

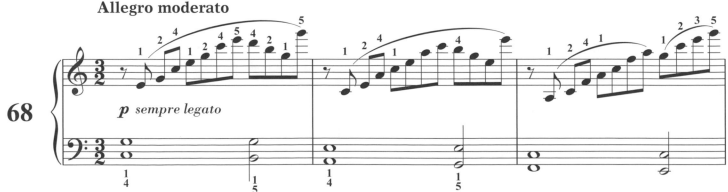

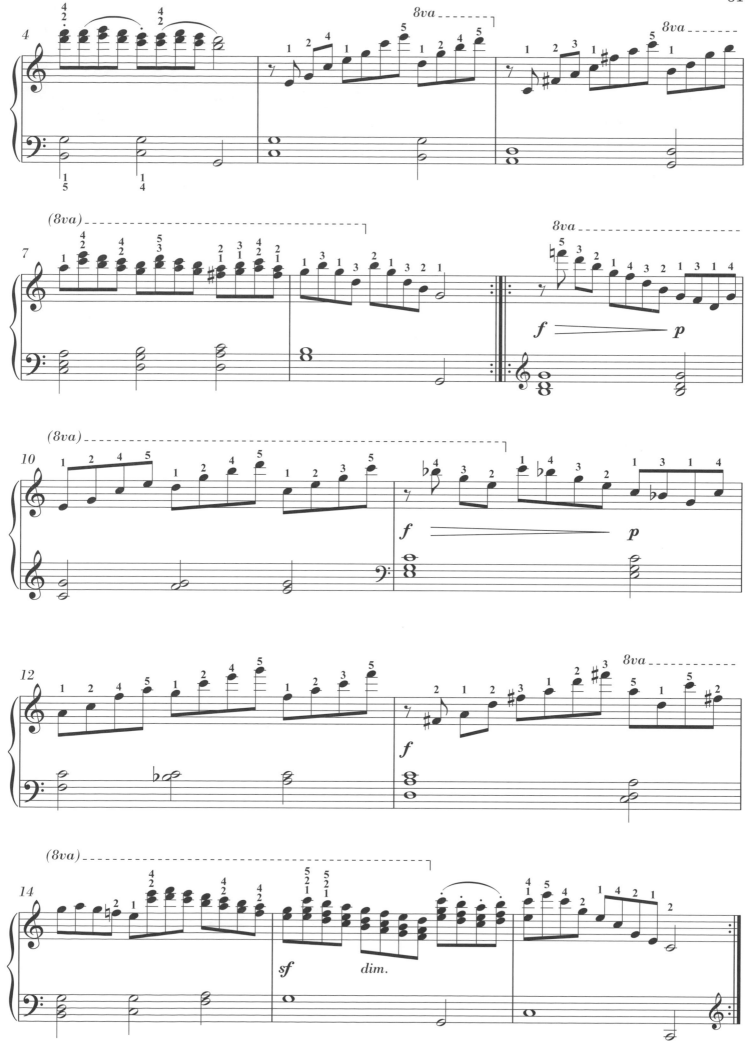

Moderato

69

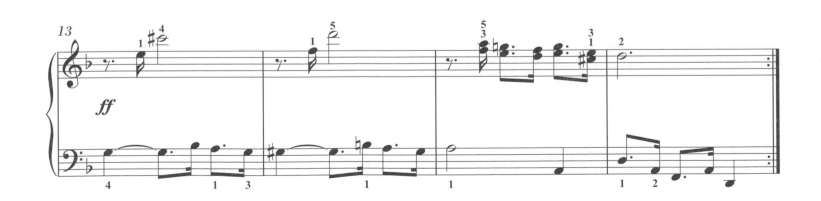

Allegro vivo e scherzando

71

Moderato quasi andantino

73

Allegro moderato

74

Allegro vivo ed energico

75

Everyday the student should play the following table from memory and tell the instructor how many sharps or flats each key has.

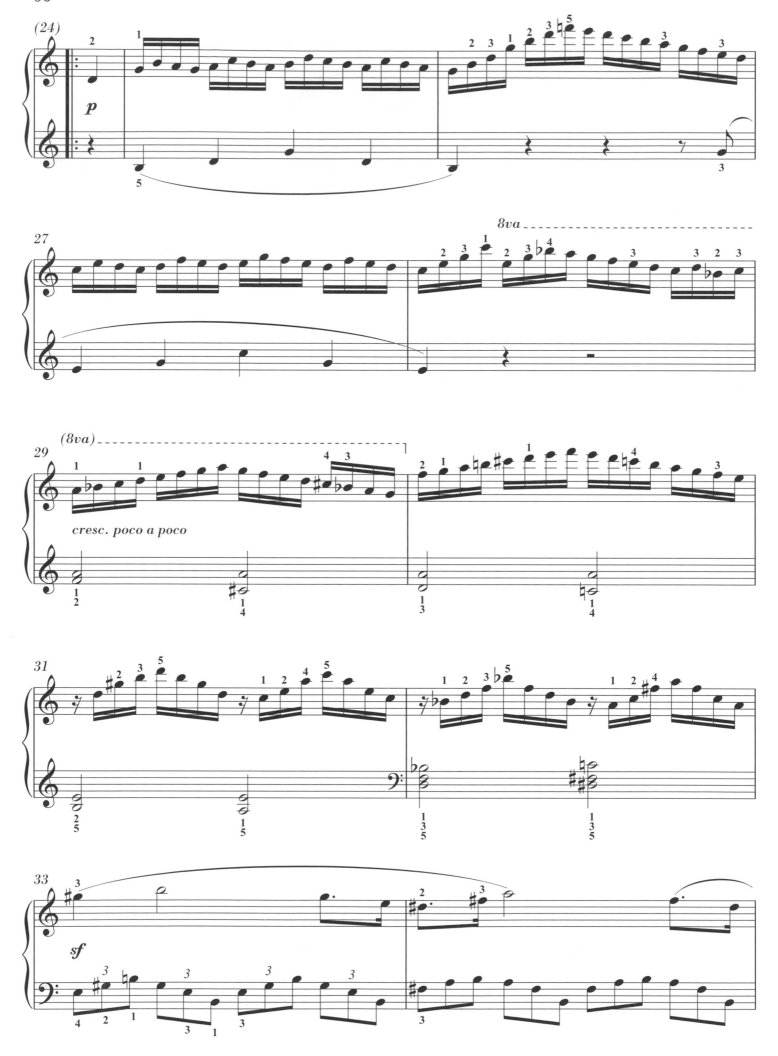

* Put both thumbs on the C.

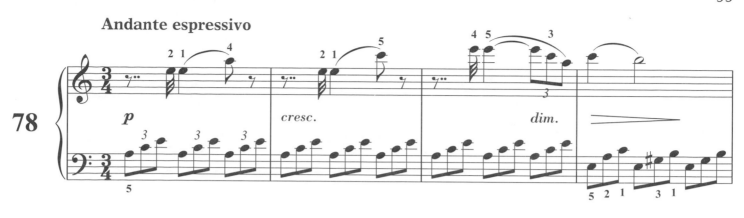

Andante espressivo

79

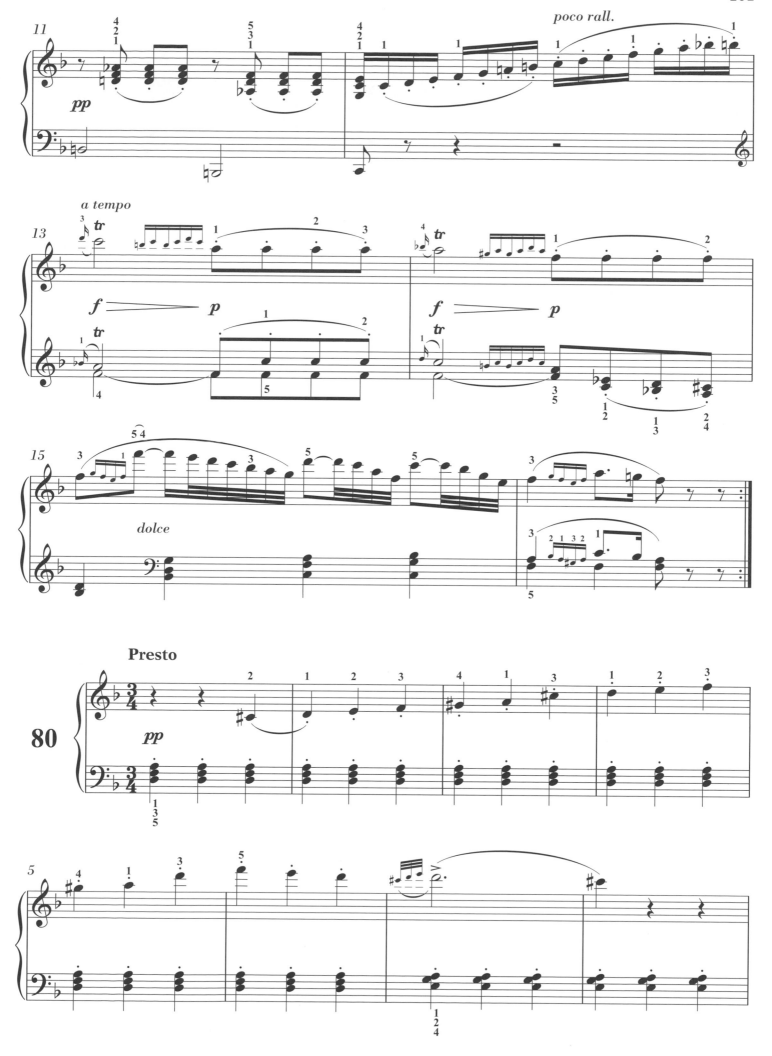

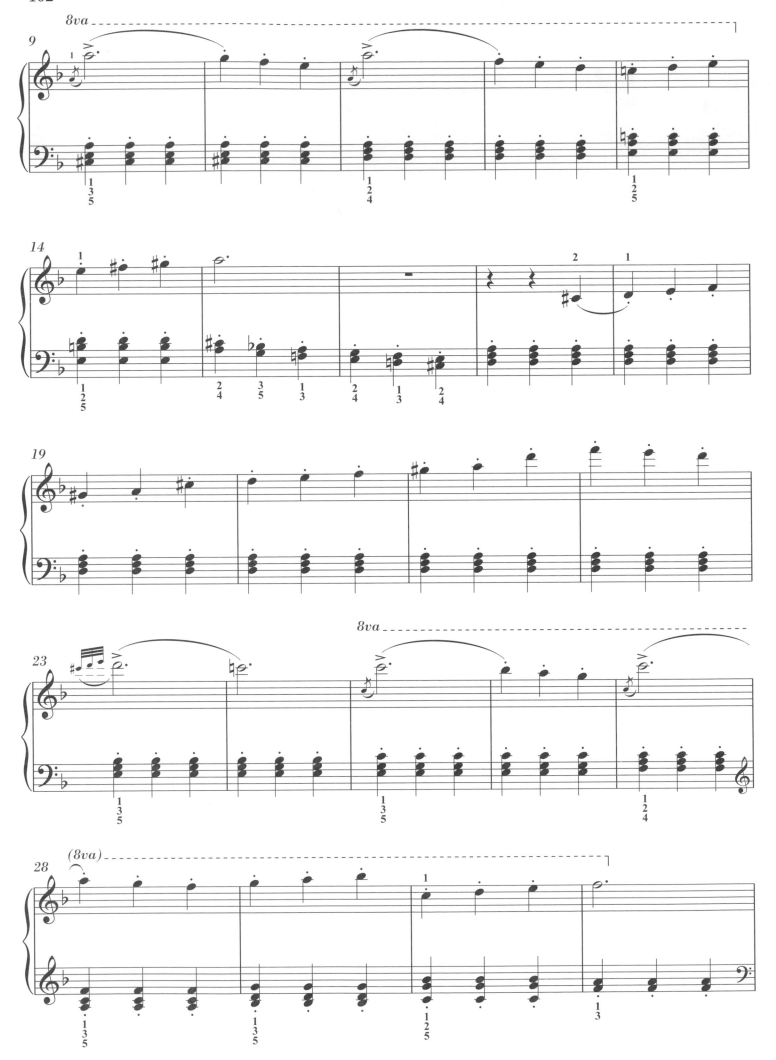

Allegretto moderato

82

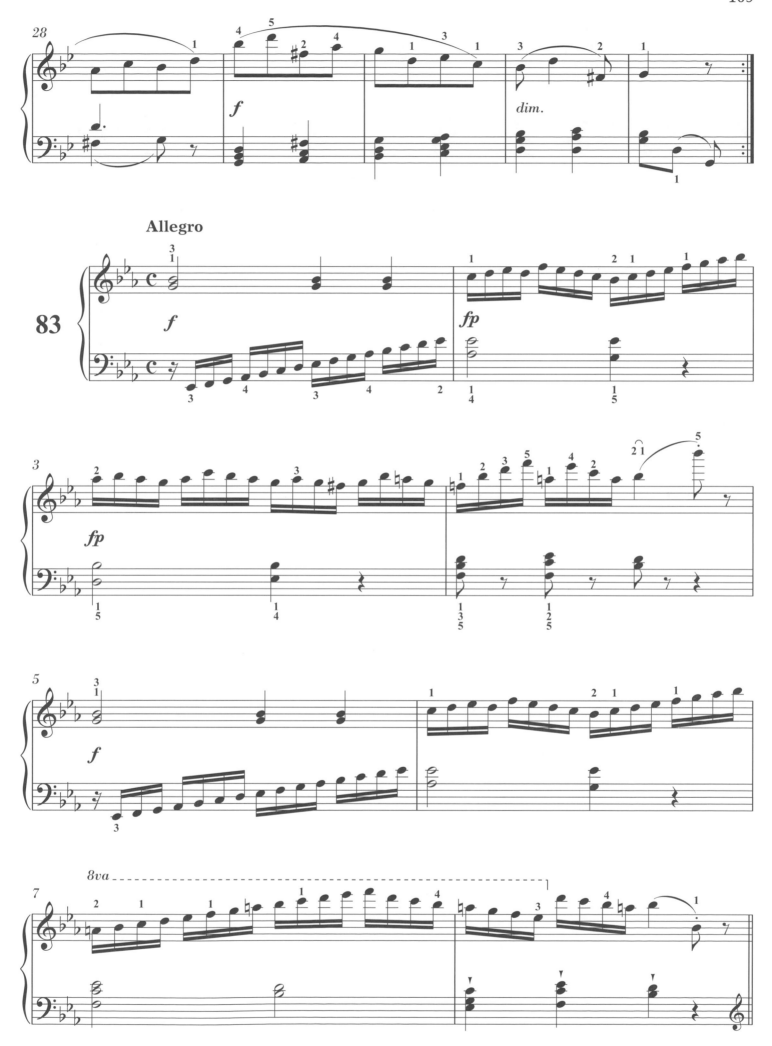

Allegro vivace

86

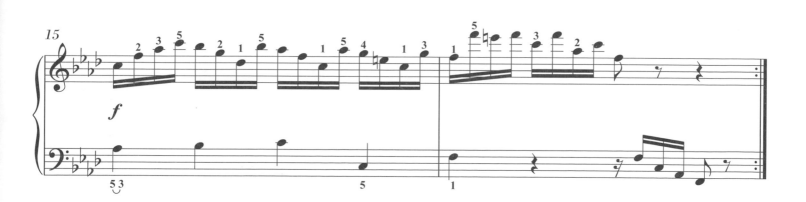

Allegro con moto ed espressivo

87

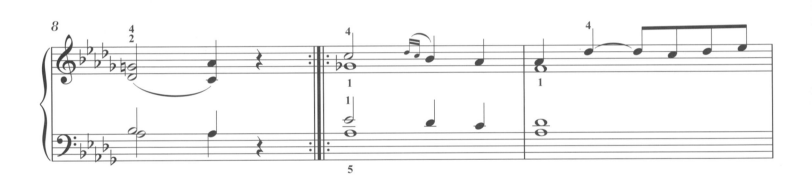

* The fingering for measures 17–32 is exactly the same as measures 1–16.

Allegro molto

88

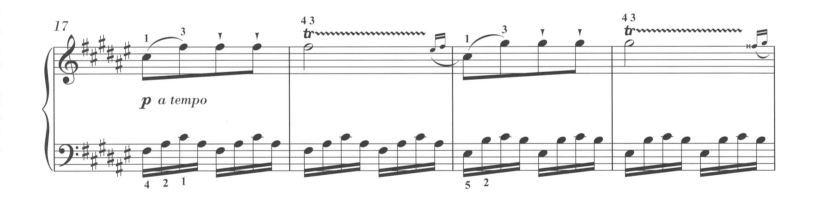

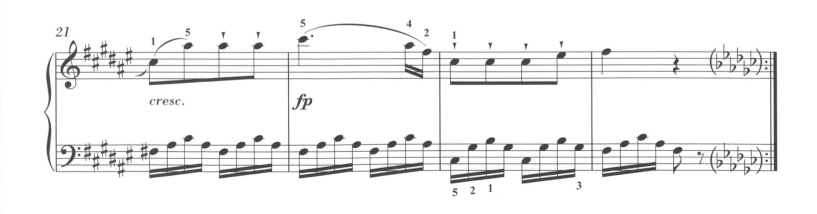

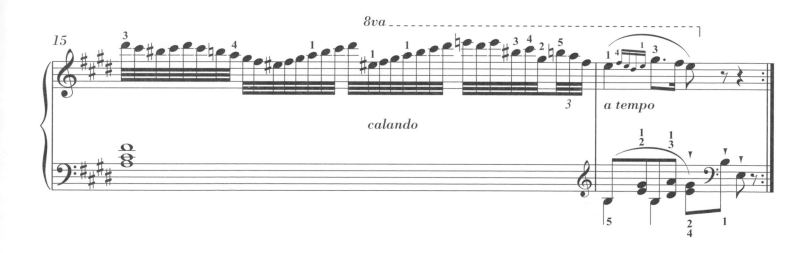

Allegro vivo

95

97

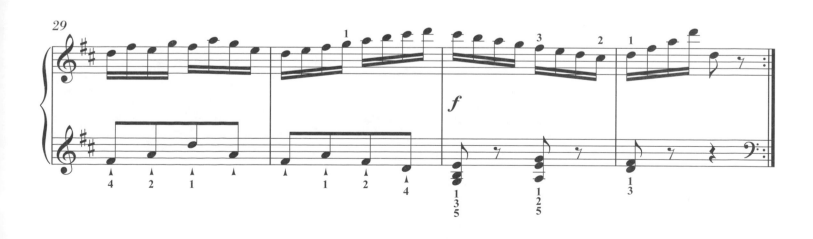

136

98

Allegro molto, quasi presto

140

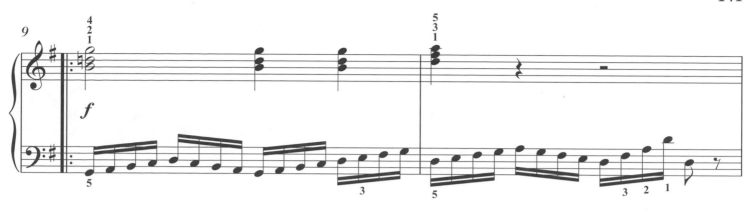

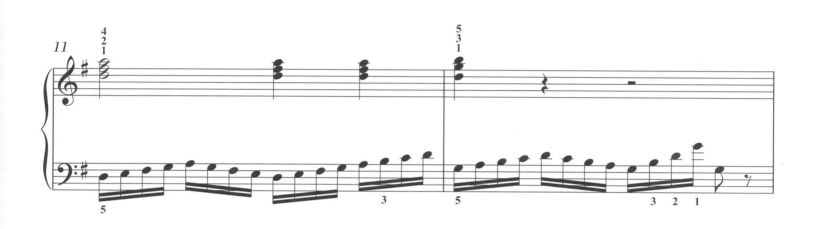

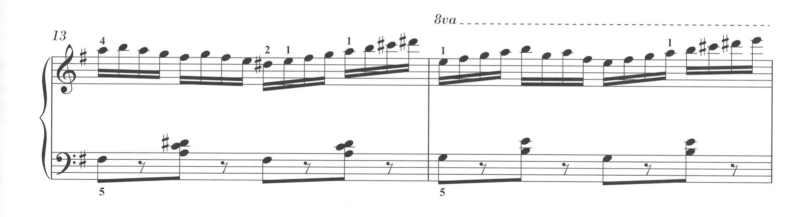